Can

of the

Great White North

Canadian Recipes of the Great White North is also for children as well as adults. With easy to do recipes your children can join in by helping and having fun with the cute illustrations drawn by Diane Lucas of Nova Scotia. My book is all about supporting children. 50% of sales will go towards the Stollery Children's Hospital Foundation. All in Memory of my daughter Jenni. This book was revised 2007.

Author: Chef Bari

Trafford Publishing
Victoria, British Columbia

For Patricia and my daughters Tianndra and Trisha

In loving memory of Jenni

Special thanks to my mom, Betty, to her husband, Peter Watts for their encouragement and love. I would also like to thank my sister, Sabrina Bell and relatives Jim and Pearl McIlveen

© Copyright 2003 Bari Demers.
All rights reserved. No part of this publication may be reproduced, stored in a retrieval system, or transmitted, in any form or by any means, electronic, mechanical, photocopying, recording, or otherwise, without the written prior permission of the author.
Published 2003 by The Canadian Northwest Company Division in conjunction with Trafford Publishing.
Second Edition 2007

http://www.trafford.com

http://chefbari.com

http://gourmetsuntours.com

http://hikingmania.com

Demers, Bari, 1956
      Canadian Recipes of the Great White North / Bari Demers;
Diana Lucas, illustrator
      1. Outdoor cookery. I. Lucas, Diane, 1959-II. Title. TX823.D44 2003 641.5'782 C2003-903315-5

Illustrations by Diane Lucas

design by Laurie Burke

Note for Librarians: A cataloguing record for this book is available from Library and Archives Canada at www.collectionscanada.ca/amicus/index-e.html
ISBN 1-4120-0536-1

PUBLISHING™
Offices in Canada, USA, Ireland and UK

Book sales for North America and international:
Trafford Publishing, 6E–2333 Government St.,
Victoria, BC V8T 4P4 CANADA
phone 250 383 6864 (toll-free 1 888 232 4444)
fax 250 383 6804; email to orders@trafford.com
Book sales in Europe:
Trafford Publishing (UK) Limited, 9 Park End Street, 2nd Floor
Oxford, UK OX1 1HH UNITED KINGDOM
phone +44 (0)1865 722 113 (local rate 0845 230 9601)
facsimile +44 (0)1865 722 868; info.uk@trafford.com
Order online at:
trafford.com/03-0905

10 9 8 7 6 5 4 3

Foreword

It is dusk; the red haze of the sun is slowly dipping below the horizon. I can smell the fresh pine, as the trees sway in the wind. The brisk fresh air is inviting to my face, as I enjoy the warmth of the crackling fire dancing in front of me. I am cooking one of my favorites— Medallions of Fresh Venison with Chanterelle Mushrooms, German pan fried potatoes and wild asparagus.

The beauty of the Canadian wilderness; how remote and wild can it be?

Just a few steps off the highways of the National Parks of Canada in Alberta, you are in raw wild country!

In the middle of the park's interior, you can experience the wild country just by taking a short hike. Be careful though, it is bear country!

In Canada's National Parks you get a chance to have a taste of nature, the raw serene wilderness at its best or worst. You become part of the wilderness, waiting for that perfect picture!

In all of this, at the end of the day, you sit beside a warm fire, enjoying entrées from **Canadian Recipes of The Great White North**.

In my book, I give you a taste of my experiences that you can prepare in you own home, at the cottage or beside your favorite campfire.

It is my pleasure to introduce to you a cookbook from the Great White Northern region—Rocky Mountain country!

My recipes can be made anywhere, enjoy them out at the cottage, on the trail or at home.

Bon appetite!

Bari Demers

Contents

Gourmet Voyageur — 8
Staples and the Great Gold Rush — 8

Wilderness Gear — 11

Appetizers — 13
Buffalo with Kinnikinnick Berry — 17

Cheddar Cheese Bannock — 19

Cajun Blue Grouse Fingers — 20

Tagliatelli con Dente di Leone — 21

Honey Cinnamon Moose Tenderloin — 23

Baked Camembert and Wild Asparagus — 24

Soups & Stocks — 26
Venison Stock — 29

Canadian French Onion & Wild Leek Soup — 30

Venison Barley Soup — 31

Blue Grouse Stock — 32

Wild Fiddlehead Soup — 33

Dolly Varden Chowder — 35

Salads — 37
Wilderness Caesar Salad — 40

Marinated Mallard Duck Salad — 42
with Blueberry Vinaigrette — 42

Hiker's Salad — 45

Entrees — 48

BBQ Moose Tenderloin & Chanterelle Mushrooms — 52

Crisp Blue Grouse Breast and Salmonberry Demi-glaze — 55

Rainbow Trout Stuffed with Rice/Buffalo Berries — 59

Tagliatelli con Pesto — 61

Hunter's Roasted Mallard Duck a l'orange stuffed with Wild Rice — 63

Tourtiere Moose Pies & Kinnikinnick Berries — 65

Ptarmigan Piccata & Herb buttered Tagliatelli — 68

Chateaubriand Stuffed with Portabella Mushrooms — 71

Madagascar Entrecote — 74

Yukon Gold Miner's Chili — 76

Time for Dessert! — 78

Grizzly Bear Claws — 81

Rocky Mountain Cookie — 83

Chocolate Moose Canadian Cake — 84

Wild Strawberry Cheesecake — 86

Home Sweet Home — 89

Tequila Lime Chicken & Shrimp Fettuccine — 92

Canadian Style Cornish Game Hen with Shitake Mushroom Sauce — 94

Canadian Northwest Company — 100

About the Author — 103

Glossary — 105

Index — 111

Gourmet Voyageur

Staples and the Great Gold Rush

In the summer of 1896 the Great Gold Rush was started from word of three men striking it rich along Rabbit Creek in the Yukon. The North West Mounted Police (now called The Royal Canadian Mounted Police) had to keep order and to help control the frenzy of unequipped gold seekers from around the world. It was ordered by the N.W.M.P. that Gold Seekers bring along a certain amount of staples with them. The reason for this was that most of the Gold Seekers coming up the Gold Rush Trail had just the shirts on their back. Many died to the harsh cold temperatures (record temperatures of -77°F) and the lack of food. It was ordered by the N.W.M.P. to have one years worth of supplies. Such items as 400 lbs Flour, 100 lbs Sugar, 200 lbs Bacon and the list went on.

It was a hard long climb up the pass, some made it, and others did not. Some went home rich and others poor. It was a stern lesson of how harsh the wilderness can be if you do not plan ahead.

The most important lesson from The Yukon Gold Rush—never enter the wilderness without some sort of staples and emergency supplies.

Today we are very fortunate when it comes to backwoods staples and supplies. They are a hundred times lighter and you have the advantage of purchasing freeze dried food items. But there still are basic staples that are required to take with you during your visit into the backwoods.

Basic Staples

Flour
Sugar

Baking Powder
Salt
Bacon
Beans
1 lb lard
Water

If you take along these basic food items, you will be safe from dehydration and hunger.

But the idea of venturing into the raw wilderness is to have fun! And for most of us, there is nothing more enjoyable than eating outdoors.

    This is where "Gourmet Voyageur Staples" comes in to the picture. Food items that add that special touch and flavour. Along with the **Basic Staple List**, here is a **Gourmet Staples List** of items to take with you into the wilderness or to your favorite cottage retreat. Along with my cookbook, **Canadian Recipes of the Great White North**, you too can create gourmet cooking in your corner of the wilderness.

Gourmet Voyageur Staples

Rice & Wild Rice
Olive Oil
Pepper
Garlic
Cornstarch
Tomato Paste
Red Wine and Port
Spices: Cajun, Dill
Cream Base
Butter & Honey
Vinegar & Red Wine Vinegar
Dijon Mustard
Potatoes

Lemons Barley

Black pepper and green peppercorns

Cream base or 33% whipping cream

I also bring along certain cheeses to add to my Gourmet Adventure. Such as Camembert cheese, grated parmesan, Swiss cheese and cheddar cheese. In any outdoors store it is easy to find packs that have inside liners to protect perishable food items. And the last item you can bring out into the wilderness are eggs—there is a special trick to this. The night before you leave on your hiking trip, crack open your egg into a freezer bag and freeze your eggs, one to each bag. Yes, you did hear right, freeze your eggs. This way, after a long day on the trail you still can make a
Wilderness Caesar Salad (page 40).

Bringing these gourmet staples you can experience the best of gourmet cooking at its best.

Gourmet Gear

When you are out in the bush, it is important to remember to bring everything retaining to small wares, or you might be using a stick to stir your cooking. Outdoor stores provide a great source of equipment for cooking that are light weight and take up little space.

With the complete list below and my cookbook, you will be on your way to making the best gourmet foods that nature has to provide. Here is the check list to help you out on your search for cooking utensils:

Utensils

tongs, wire whip, wooden spoons, paring knife or hunting knife, cooking fork, flipper or off-set metal spatula and plastic spatula

Pots

sauce pan, frying pan, large, medium & small pots

Other Equipment

Retractable reflector oven
Grill (used for BBQ's on top of the campfire coals)
Oven mitts
Metal strainer
Stainless steel assorted bowls

Wilderness Gear

When you enter any wild country, you had better be prepared for the worst. As beautiful nature is, it is also unforgiving. All it takes is one forgotten item or one mistake, to turn your exploring expedition into a disaster that may lead to death!

In this section, I have provided a detailed check list before you attempt to take a hike into your neck of the woods. It is best to have these items in your backpack at all times—even for that short mountain trip for the day. You just never know what might happen.

Clothing
Inner Layer

Bring along clothing items that give the layering effect.
First layer: a thermal or polypropylene layer that allow moisture to seep through and dry.
Second layer: you require a sleeved shirt that is made of wool or flannel to allow you to retain warmth.
Third layer: a fleece sweater or fleece underline jacket that can retain warmth and repel outer moisture. And do not forget warm light weight outdoor socks. Bring along several pairs!

Outer Layer: *Jackets*

Again, use the layering effect when choosing outdoor clothing. You can choose between two and three layer jackets that are of Gore-Tex material. I always choose three layer jackets, because you never know when you might be facing freezing temperatures in the mountains. Do not forget, gloves or mitts and a warm fleece hat.

Emergency & Must-have Items

Matches and weather proof lighter, sun screen, insect repellent, magnify glass, hunting knife or folding knife, high energy food bars, freeze dried food items, water, flashlight, emergency blanket, first aid kit, hot pads, flares, snare wire, nylon rope, mesh for catching fish, string, whistle, compass(get to know how to use it), map of area, tracker or emergency strobe.

Items that would add to safety

Emergency signal markers, night light sticks and folding shovel.

Appetizers

NOTES: http://chefbari.com

Appetizers

The first appetizer was commonly used by North American Indians, such as the Blackfoot, Assiniboine, Cree, Stoney Plain, Bella Coola, Chilcotin, Okanagan and Thompson, to name a few. All used the kinnikinnick berry to mix with their dried buffalo. This made a flavourable buffalo jerky for the hard winters ahead. They also used the leaves of the kinnikinnick plant as a form of tobacco.

    North American Indians were very resourceful when it came to using plants from Mother Earth, and today we all can have the opportunity to use plants to make great dishes by our own campfire.

Buffalo with Kinnikinnick Berry

What is great about this appetizer is that you can make it at home and bring it on the trail.

Yield: 4 servings
Ingredients :
½ piece buffalo inside round (5lbs)
2 cups /500ml kinnikinnick berries
½ cup /125ml water
1 tbsp/15ml red wine
¾ cup/175ml sugar
¼ cup/50ml olive oil

Method:
At medium heat, place your favorite skillet over a campfire or on top of a stove.

Add in the sugar, red wine, water and kinnikinnick berries. Let cook to a thicken syrup. Remove from heat and let cool.

Slice the buffalo inside round into long thin pieces.

Take half of the sauce and place in a shallow pan. Place in raw pieces of buffalo and let marinade for a couple of hours (better to marinate all night if you are at home.)

Out at the camp site, or at home, you can place the marinated piece of kinnikinnick buffalo in a hot frying pan with a touch of olive oil. Cook both sides on low heat, being careful not to burn.

Violaˆ; there you have it—your first appetizer!

Substitutions

Buffaloinsideround—insideroundofbeef
kinnikinnickberry—raspberries

Appetizers

You can't go into the woods without making some kind of bannock. This appetizer is great by itself or with a hardy dish, such as Bison Chili.

Cheddar Cheese Bannock

Ingredients

2	cups / 500	ml	flour
½	cup / 125	ml	lard
1	tbsp / 15	ml	baking powder
1	tsp / 5	ml	salt
2	tbsp / 30	ml	grated cheddar cheese
1	cup / 250	ml	water

Method

Take a medium size bowl and place in the flour, salt, baking powder. Mix together. Cut up the lard into cubes and mix by hand into the flour mixture.

Add half of the water and mix again. Be careful not to over mix. Add the rest of the water and grated cheddar cheese; form into a ball.

Cut into four pieces and roll each piece into a long pencil shape. Wrap around a green pine stick and cook over a fire with hot coals.

Or, if at home, place on a baking sheet and place in the oven at

350°F for 10–15 minutes, until a nice golden brown.

If you ever were out hunting, somewhere, somehow, you will meet up with one species of grouse. The most common one that I found was blue spruce grouse. How did they come up with that name? Well, you would find them up in the blue spruce trees, trying to hide from us. They are so dumb; all you have to do is throw a rock at them. And, if you are a good shot ... you have dinner.

Cajun Blue Grouse Fingers

Yield: 4 servings

Ingredients

2 4 oz / 125 g blue grouse breasts sliced into strips
1 tbsp / 15 ml Cajun spice

Dipping Sauce

1 cup / 250 ml wild blueberries
¼ cup / 50 ml sugar

Method

Take your strips of blue grouse and pound them out flat. Mix together with Cajun spice. Place in a skillet and cook both sides until done. Set on middle of plate.

In the same skillet, add the blue berries and sugar. Cook until a thick syrup. Place on the side of your dish and dip the Cajun Blue Grouse Fingers. Enjoy!

Substitutions

Blue grouse strips— chicken strips

Appetizers

This appetizer is best prepared at home or at the cottage. Or, just bring along your favorite pasta on the trail. Tagliatelli is like fettuccine.

Tagliatelli con Dente di Leone

Yield: 4 servings

Ingredients

2½ cups / 625 ml flour
3 whole eggs
1 tbsp / 15 ml olive oil
2 cloves garlic, minced
1 bunch baby dandelions
salt & pepper to taste

parmesan cheese to taste

Method

Place flour on a board and make a well in the middle. Crack your eggs into the middle and a pinch of salt. Form into stiff dough, adding water if required. Take the dough and roll out to a thickness of $^1/16''$ (thin). Cut into strips of ⅛" width and place out to dry. My grandfather (a true Italian) would place the strips of noodles on a broomstick to dry.

Next, take a medium size pot with water and a pinch of salt. Place it on top a grate under campfire coals. Bring to a boil and add your dry homemade tagliatelli noodles.

Cook until al dente'. Place in cold water to stop the cooking process.

Cut the baby dandelions into thin strips. Take a sauté pan with olive oil and place on top of a grate under campfire coals. Add your baby dandelions and minced garlic. Quick sauté and add your pasta. Sauté again, a pinch of salt—and you are ready for the taste of your life—bon appetite! Grate a healthy portion of parmesan cheese on top.

Substitutions

babydandelions—babyspinach
tagliatelli—fettuccine

Appetizers

Honey Cinnamon Moose Tenderloin

Yield: 4 servings

Ingredients

4	oz	/ 125	g	moose tenderloin
1	tsp	/ 5	ml	cinnamon
½	tsp	/ 2	ml	Cajun spice
¼	cup	/ 50	ml	red wine
3	tbsp	/ 45	ml	honey

8 thin pine sticks or skewers

Method

Thinly slice your moose tenderloin into ⅛" thickness. Weave each slice onto its own pine stick (pine stick adds it own flavor) or skewer. Prepare a marinade of Cajun spice, red wine and honey. Mix all together and place the moose tenders in the marinade and let stand until the next day.

Take out the moose tenders and set aside. Mix together one tablespoon of marinade with rest of honey and cinnamon. Brush the mixture onto both sides of the moose tenders and place on the barbecue. Cook to perfection and take a bite!

Substitutions

Moose tenderloin— Beef Tenderloin

When I lived in the Okanagan Valley, I found wild asparagus all along the hillsides.

Baked Camembert and Wild Asparagus

Yield: 4 servings

Ingredients

1	cup / 250	ml	flour
2	tbsp / 30	ml	canola oil
½	cup / 125	ml	warm water
½	tsp / 2	ml	baking powder
8	pieces		wild asparagus
2	oz / 50	g	Camembert cheese

Method

Mix together flour and baking powder in a medium size bowl. Add the oil to the warm water and slowly mix into the flour mixture. Your finished product should pull away from the bowl. Dry and yet still sticky. Place dough on a flat board and roll out to ⅛ ″ thick. Set to the side and let rest.

Bring water to a boil in a saucepan and add the raw wild asparagus. Cook for only three minutes or until they are bright green. Remove and cool down in cold water (not hard to find here in the wilderness.)

Lay out you dough and cut into four even squares. Place on thinly sliced Camembert cheese and place in the middle of each square. Lay on top two wild asparagus for each square. Roll up the squares and pinch each side to make sure the cheese does not ooze out. Bake under a reflector oven for ten minutes under medium heat or 350°F in an oven.

Substitutions
There really isn't a good substitution for this one.

Soups & Stocks

Notes:

Soups and Stocks

Soups and stocks are best prepared at home or at the cottage. But what I have done is take them out on the trail frozen. They are good to warm up over a campfire during winter or fall hikes.

Venison Stock Yield: 20 servings

Ingredients

2	lbs / 1	kg	venison bones
3	medium		carrots
1	large		onion
1	whole		wild leek
2	cups / 500	ml	red wine
2	whole		bay leaves
1	whole		rosemary leaf

salt & pepper to taste
water - enough to fill the pot

Method

Take a large pot and place on top of the stove. Put all the above ingredients into the pot and cover with water until the bones are covered. Bring to a boil and then let simmer for four to six hours, depending on your taste of the venison.

Now you are ready to use the stock for your soups and sauces!

Substitutions

venison bones— beef bones

Canadian French Onion & Wild Leek Soup

Yield: 4 servings

Ingredients

4 whole sweet white onions, sliced

2 whole wild leeks, sliced ½ cup / 125 ml

red wine 4 cups / 1 kg

venison stock - 4 cups

2 tbsp / 30 ml tomato paste

1 garlic clove, minced

1 cup / 250 ml shredded Swiss cheese

salt & pepper to taste

Method

Take a heavy pot and place it on top of the stove under medium heat.

Add the sliced onions, garlic and leeks. Sauté until blonde in colour. Add tomato paste and red wine.

Pour in the venison stock and bring to a boil. Reduce heat and let simmer for one hour. Add more venison stock if required and season to taste.

Ladle the soup into French onion bowls and top with shredded Swiss cheese. Place in oven or beside the campfire coals for a couple of minutes. Serve, but be careful—it is hot.

Nothing better than hot soup on a cold night!

Soups and Stocks

Venison Barley Soup

Yield: 4 servings

Ingredients

½ lb / 250	g	venison, cubed
3 medium		potatoes, medium cut
3 medium		carrots, small cut
1	ml	wild leek, sliced
3 tbsp / 45		olive oil
2 cloves		garlic, minced
¼ cup / 50	ml	barley, soaked in 1 cup / 250 ml of water overnight
8 cups /	litre	venison stock
1 ½ tsp / 2	ml	rosemary

salt & pepper to taste

Method

Place your medium size pot with olive oil on top of the stove. Add the venison and sauté for ten minutes. Add your carrots, garlic and leek. Sauté for three minutes. Add the potatoes and again sauté for three minutes. Add all of the venison stock, barley and rosemary. Bring to a boil. Reduce heat and let simmer for one hour. Add salt and pepper to

taste. There you have it—enjoy!

Substitutions

venison— beef

Blue Grouse Stock

Yield: 20 servings

Ingredients

2 lbs / 1 kg blue grouse bones
3 medium carrots
1 large onion
1 wild leek
2 cups / 500 ml white wine
2 bay leaves
salt & pepper to taste
water

Method

Take a large pot and place it on top of a stove. Put in all the above and top with water until the bones are covered. Bring to a boil and then let simmer for four to six hours, depending on your taste of the stock.

Now you are ready to use the stock in soups and sauces.

Substitutions

blue grouse bones—chicken bones

Soups and Stocks

Wild Fiddlehead Soup

Yield: 4 servings

Ingredients

½ lb / 500 g wild fiddleheads
2 cloves garlic, minced
1 whole wild leek, sliced
¼ cup / 150 ml olive oil
¼ cup / 50 ml flour
8 cups / 2 litres grouse stock
1 cup / 250 ml 33% cream
salt & pepper to taste
grated Camembert (optional)

Method

Place a medium size pot with water and a pinch of salt, on top of the stove. Bring to a boil and add the fiddleheads. Cook for two minutes and place in cold water, to stop the cooking process.

Retain 1 cup of the boiling water and set aside.

Take half of the fiddleheads to the cutting board and slice into thin strips.

Take the empty pot and add the olive oil. Put in the wild leek and garlic, sauté for a couple of minutes.

Add your strips of fiddleheads and sauté for one minute.

Add the flour to the mixture and stir in evenly. Cook for five minutes, stirring it frequently.

Add your stock and the one cup of water. Bring to a simmer, cook for ten minutes. Add salt and pepper to taste.

Take off the fire; add your cream and the rest of fiddleheads.

And you are ready to serve.

Add some grated Camembert cheese on top and you will have the best cream soup ever!

Soups and Stocks

Dolly Varden Chowder

Yield: 4 servings

Ingredients:
Fish Stock
½ lb / 500ml fish bones
1 fresh   lemon
1   dill weed
1 tbsp/ 15 ml black peppercorns

Chowder:
1 tbsp/ 15ml olive oil
2 medium   carrots (small cut)
2 medium   peeled potatoes (medium cubed)
2 medium   leeks (sliced thin)
2 cloves   garlic, minced
1/2lb / 500 ml bacon (small cut)
1 dolly varden (skin and bones removed and cut into cubes)
¼ cup / 50 ml flour
8 cups / 2 litres fish stock
1 cup / 250 ml (33%) cream

Method
Fish Stock
    Add all the fish stock ingredients into a large pot and fill with water to coverthe bones. Place on top of the stove. Bring to a boil and let simmer for 45 minutes. Strain.

Chowder
Take a medium size pot and place in the olive oil and bacon. Cook until bacon is done.

Add carrots, garlic and leeks and cook for five minutes.

Add potatoes and sauté for another five minutes. Put in the cubed Dolly Varden and flour; stir slowly not to break up the Fish. Cook until the Dolly Varden is half cooked.

Pour in the fish stock, stir and bring to a simmer. Cook for 20 minutes, simmering constantly.

Take off fire and add cream.

Substitutions

fresh Dolly Varden—fresh salmon

Salads

Notes: http://bari.gourmetsuntours.com

Salads

In the wilderness there is an abundance of edible plants ready for the taking. The most common ones, and easy to notice, are dandelion and plantain leaves. In both cases, each plant must be picked when the leaves are young. Otherwise they become very tough and fibrous.

Wilderness Caesar Salad

Yield: 4 servings

Ingredients

½	lb	/ 500	ml	baby plantain
1	cup / 250		ml	olive oil
2	cloves			garlic, minced
1	whole			egg
½	tsp	/ 2	ml	Dijon mustard
2	tsp	/ 10	ml	vinegar
½	fresh			lemon, squeezed
1	cup / 250		ml	fresh parmesan cheese

salt & pepper to taste

Method

Wash the baby plantain in cold water, remove the stem. Set to the side.

Now is the time to take your not so frozen egg out of its freezer bag

(see page 10 for details.) Add the garlic, Dijon mustard, and vinegar to the egg. Squeeze in lemon. Hold the bowl rigid and whip the mixture. Slowly drizzle in the olive oil.

Add salt and pepper to taste.

Place the baby plantain in a bowl and add the Caesar dressing to your taste.

Top with fresh grated parmesan cheese.

Substitutions

baby plantain (There are two different region kinds of plantain. In South America there is a well known plant that most relate to as plantain, which resembles a banana. But, the plantain in the Northwest Region of Canada is more related to a hearty leaf spinach and is very common throughout the Canadian plains — its close substitute is spinach.

Salads

When I was a kid, I remember fishing out at Shuswap Falls, just west of Lumby, B.C. in the North Okanagan Valley. While I was waiting for a fish I would usually sit beside a bush of wild blueberries.

Nothing better than a handful of fresh wild blueberries. Just make sure you make a lot of noise first, before approaching a berry bush. You just might run into a bear. I always let the bear have the right of way for good reason.

Marinated Mallard Duck Salad with Blueberry Vinaigrette

This salad is best prepared at home or at the cottage.

Yield: 4 servings

Ingredients
Salad

1 cup / 250 ml white wine
2 mallard duck breasts
1 clove garlic minced
2 tbsp / 30 ml olive oil

Wild mix greens (mix of baby dandelion and plantain leaves)

4 cups / 1 litre tagliatelli (see page 68)
1 cup / 250 ml fresh shredded parmesan cheese
salt & pepper to taste

Vinaigrette

1 cup / 250 ml fresh wild blueberries
½ cup / 125 ml olive oil
¼ cup / 50 ml vinegar
2 tbsp / 30 ml sugar

Method

In a bowl, put in white wine, minced garlic and olive oil. Butterfly the mallard breasts into four pieces and place into bowl. Let marinate over night.

Next day, place the butterfly mallard on the barbecue and cook until done. Salt and pepper to taste.

To make the vinaigrette: crush half of the blueberries into a bowl, mix together with the vinegar, sugar and olive oil.

It is time to plate: In the middle of the plate, add the tagliatelli. Place on top a generous portion of wild mix greens. Slice the piece of mallard breast into strips and place evenly on top of the salad.

Drizzle on the vinaigrette and sprinkle on the rest of the fresh wild blueberries and a generous portion of fresh shredded parmesan cheese.

Substitutions

Mallard duck—domestic duck

Salads

Hiker's Salad

Yield: 4 servings
Ingredients:
1/2lb /250 g   wild mix greens (mixture of baby dandelion & plantain leaves)
1 cup/250ml cooked bacon bits
2 BBQ Blue grouse breasts (cubed)
½ cup/125ml olive oil
2 garlic cloves minced
2 tbsp/30ml vinegar
1 cup/250ml fresh shredded parmesan cheese
Salt & Pepper to taste

Method:

Place the wild mix salad in a bowl and add the bacon bits and cooked, cubed blue grouse breasts.

In a separate container, mix together the olive oil, vinegar, garlic and salt and pepper to taste. Add to the mix salad and toss.

Place on your favorite large plate and top generously with fresh parmesan cheese. Violaˆ—bon appetite!

Substitutions

Blue grouse chicken breasts—chicken breasts

wild mix greens—baby spinach

Notes: http://gourmetsuntours.com

More Notes:

Entrées

Recipe Conversion Chart

One stick of butter is 1/4 pound or about 110 grams.
Butter in the US is sold in one pound boxes, each box containing 4 sticks.

Decimals
0.25 = 1/4
0.33 = 1/3
0.50 = 1/2
0.66 = 2/3
0.75 = 3/4

Pound, cups, tablespoon and teaspoon conversions assume the base weight-volume of water
1 pound = 2 cups
1 ounce = 2 tablespoons
1 tablespoon = 3 teaspoons = 0.5 oz = 15 grams
1 teaspoon = 0.17 oz = 5 grams
pinch is less than 1/8 teaspoon
dl = deciliter = 1/10 of a liter = 1/2 cup

Weight-volume of:
Flour: 1 pound = 3 1/2 cups
Sugar: 1 pound = 2 1/4 cups

c = cup
t = tsp = teaspoon
T = tbsp = tablespoon
C = Celsius
F = Fahrenheit
g = gr = gram
kg = kilogram

Metric Conversion Chart

US	Canadian	Australian
1/4 tsp	1 mL	1 ml
1/2 tsp	2 mL	2 ml
1 tsp	5 mL	5 ml
1 Tbl	15 mL	20 ml
1/4 cup	50 mL	60 ml
1/3 cup	75 mL	80 ml
1/2 cup	125 mL	125 ml
2/3 cup	150 mL	170 ml
3/4 cup	175 mL	190 ml
1 cup	250 mL	250 ml
1 quart	1 liter	1 litre

Entrees

Bbq Moose Tenderloin & Chanterelle Mushrooms
with German pan-fried potatoes & asparagus

Yield: 4 servings

Ingredients

BBQ Moose Tenderloin with Chanterelle Mushrooms

    4 pieces moose tenderloin, ¼" thick
    3 tbsp / 45 ml olive oil
    2 tsp / 10 ml butter
    ½ wild leek, thin sliced
    3 cups / 750 ml chanterelle mushrooms
    2 cloves garlic, minced
    ¼ cup / 50 ml red wine
    1 cup / 250 ml 33% cream or cream base and add

                      Purified water if out on the trail
    salt & pepper to taste

Pan-fried potatoes & wild asparagus

    4 large potatoes, unpeeled
    ¼ cup / 50 ml olive oil
    2 whole wild leeks, thin sliced
    1 clove garlic, minced
    1 tbsp / 15 ml wild dill weed
    ¼ lb / 125 g wild asparagus
    3 tbsp / 45 ml butter

salt & pepper to taste

Method

begin with the pan-fried potatoes

Slice your raw potatoes to ⅛" thick and place in a medium pot. Fill with water covering the potatoes, place on the coals in the campfire. Bring to a boil and let cook for five minutes.

Drain and place potatoes in cold water. Set aside.

In a frying pan, add 1½ tablespoons of butter, ¼ cup of olive oil. Set your frying pan on top of a grate and under campfire coals or on top of a stove.

Divide your sliced potatoes into thirds, add one third at a time to the frying pan. Add a pinch of dill weed and garlic each time.

Cook each side of the potato until golden brown. Salt and pepper to taste.

Set to the side on a warmer when finished.

begin with the moose tenderloin

Lightly season and oil the moose tenderloins with a touch of olive oil and Cajun spice.

Place on top of the barbecue and cook to your liking.

Take a frying pan and place on top of a grate under campfire coals (or on top of your stove.)

Put in the olive oil and butter and melt.

Add the wild leek, garlic and chanterelle mushrooms.

Note: Notice that I did not say wild chanterelle mushrooms. It is safer to obtain your chanterelle mushrooms from your grocery store, than risk the possibility of being poisoned from wild mushrooms.

Add red wine and sauté for five minutes, or until the moisture of the mushrooms has evaporated.

Pour in cream and let reduce until a thick sauce. Set to the side.

Take a small sauce pot with water and bring to a boil. Add your wild asparagus and cook for three minutes or until al dente'. Drain and cover with butter and salt and pepper.

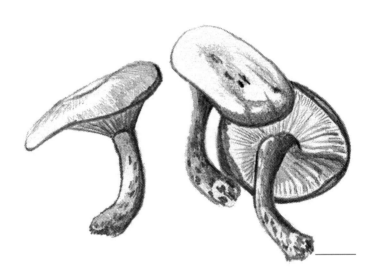

To the Plate

In the middle of your plate evening lay out your German fried potatoes in a half moon.

In the middle of the half moon place two pieces of cooked moose tenderloin. Drizzle with the chanterelle sauce.

On top of the tenderloin lay across the wild asparagus in an "x" formation.

And there you have it; all there is left to do is enjoy!

Substitutions

Moose tenderloin— Beef tenderloin

Crisp Blue Grouse Breasts and Salmonberry Demi-glaze
with wild rice & buttered fiddleheads

Yield: 4 servings

Ingredients

8 whole blue grouse breasts

2 cups / 500 ml wild salmonberries

¼ cup / 50 ml flour

¼ wild leek, finely chopped

2 cloves garlic, minced

¼ cup / 50 ml olive oil

2 cups / 500 ml blue grouse stock (see page 32)

2 cups / 500 ml dry bread crumbs

1 tsp / 5 ml dry rosemary leaf

1 tbsp / 15 ml Cajun spice

¼ cup / 50 ml Dijon mustard

¼ cup / 50 ml red wine

½ cup / 125 ml long grain rice

¼ cup / 50 ml wild rice

4 cups / 1 litre wild fiddleheads

2 tbsp / 30 ml butter salt & pepper to taste

Method

Place the dry breadcrumbs into a stainless steel bowl. Add in the Cajun spice and crush the rosemary herb. Salt and pepper to taste. Mix together. Soak the blue grouse breasts in the red wine and place into the bread crumb mixture. Pat each side to make sure it is well coated. Put the olive oil in a frying pan on top of a grate and heat under campfire coals. Brown each side and take out of frying pan. Place in reflector oven to cook until done.

Join Chef Bari Gourmet Fun in the Sun Club at http://chefbari.com

Entrées
Prepare your rice

In a small saucepan, take the wild rice and fill with water just to cover. Set on top of the grate under campfire coals (or on top of the stove.) Bring to a boil and bring back to a simmer. Let cook for twenty minutes or until the wild rice swells. Do the same with the long grain rice. Mix each rice together and add one tablespoon of butter. Salt and pepper to taste.

Prepare the Sauce

In a sauce pan, put 1 tablespoon of olive oil and place on top of the grate over campfire coals. Place in the finely chopped wild leek and garlic. Pour in the 3 tablespoons of the red wine and let reduce. Add the rest of the olive oil and stir in the flour with a wooden spoon. Keep stirring and cook until a golden brown.

Pour in the stock and stir with a wire whip. Let cook and simmer for ten minutes. Bring to the thickness of your choice. If required, add more stock to thin sauce. When the sauce is to the right consistency, then add one cup of the salmonberries. Let cook for another five minutes. Set to the side.

Put a saucepan with water on top of the grate under the campfire coals. Bring to a boil and add the fiddleheads. Let cook for five minutes and drain. Add the rest of the butter, season with salt and pepper to taste.

To the Plate

In the middle of the plate place some of the rice, which can be formed by using a cup. Beside the rice, pour a nice portion of sauce. Place on top of the sauce, two crispy blue grouse breasts. On the other side of the rice, place on the fiddleheads. Bon ap petit!

Substitutions

Blue grouse breasts— chicken breasts
salmonberry— raspberry

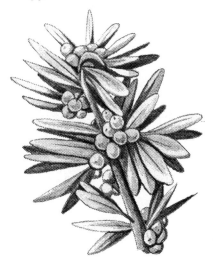

Entrées

Rainbow Trout stuffed with Long Grain Rice & Buffalo Berries

The stuffing is best prepared before you leave home, because the only place I know where to find buffalo berries is in the southern part of Saskatewan. You head down to an area called Frenchman River. On the shoreline banks you will find large bushes with thorns.

Yield: 4–6 servings

Ingredients

¼	cup / 50	ml	white wine
2	2 lb / 500	g	whole rainbow trout, cleaned
1	whole		lemon
½	lb / 125	g	fresh buffalo berries
½	cup / 125	ml	water
½	cup / 125	ml	olive oil
2	cloves		garlic, minced
2	tbsp / 30	ml	butter
2	tsp / 10	ml	dill weed
2	cups / 500	ml	grouse stock

½	cup / 125	ml	long grain rice
1	medium		carrot, small cut
1	medium		onion, small cut
2	cups / 500	ml	33% cream or cream base with water

Method

preparing the rice pilaf

Take a medium size pot and place on top of the stove. Add ¼ cup of the olive oil and one tablespoon of butter. Put in the onions and carrots. Sauté for three minutes. Put in the rice and stir with a wooden spoon for another three minutes. Add the stock and buffalo berries and bring to a boil.

Set in the oven and let cook for thirty minutes. After it is ready, let cool. This can be prepared the day before. It is very important to have the cooked rice cold before proceeding to the fish.

Preparing the Rainbow Trout

Make sure the trout is clean and washed in cold water before proceeding. It is best to debone the inside of the trout, but it is not necessary. At home get your local supermarket meat cutter to debone it for you.

Form the rice and buffalo berry mixture into four even oval balls. Squeeze lemon into the open cavity of the trout and add the rice and buffalo berry mixture. Close the trout tightly and tie together with string.

Put on a frying pan, with the rest of the olive oil, on top of the grill. Pan fry each trout on both sides. Place in the reflector oven and let cook for ten minutes or until the trout is done (depending on the amount of heat.) If made at home, place in oven at 400°F for ten minutes.

Preparing the Sauce

In a saucepan pour in your cream and 1 tsp of dill weed. Place on the top of the grill and let cook until slightly thick. At the last moment whip in ¼ cup of white wine. Let reduce.

To the Plate

If you do not want the skin of the trout, remove it. I do it for presentation and to remove the bitter taste of the cooked skin. Take a sharp knife and cut the trout into thick slices of four in the middle of the plate. Drizzle on the wild dill sauce. On the side serve Wilderness Caesar Salad (page 40.)

Enjoy this treat!

Tagliatelli con Pesto

This pasta is best prepared at home or at the cottage.

Yield: 2 servings

Ingredients

2½ cups / 625		ml	flour
3	whole		eggs
2	tbsp / 30	ml	olive oil
3	cloves		garlic, minced
½	cup / 125	ml	wild pine nuts, finely chopped
¼	cup / 50	ml	fresh basil, finely chopped
2	cups / 500	ml	33% cream

salt & pepper to taste

parmesan cheese to taste

Method

Place flour on a board and make a well in the middle. Crack your eggs into the middle and add a pinch of salt. Form into stiff dough, adding water if required. Take the dough and roll out to a thickness of $1/16''$ (thin). Cut into strips of $1/8''$ width and place out to dry.

In a frying pan add the olive oil, fresh basil and pine nuts. Place on top of the grate under coals of the campfire. Sauté until roasted to a light brown. The pesto is ready for the next step.

Take a medium size pot with water and a pinch of salt. Place it on top a grate under campfire coals. Bring to a boil and add your dry homemade noodles. Cook until al dente.

Place in bowl and mix with the pesto. Plate and top with fresh grated parmesan cheese. Season to taste. Add a sprig of fresh basil on top and enjoy!

Hunter's Roasted Mallard Duck ˆ l'orange stuffed with Wild Rice

Yield: 4 servings

Ingredients

1	whole		mallard duck, cleaned
6	whole		oranges
1	cup / 250	ml	sugar
2	tbsp / 30	ml	butter
1	cup / 250	ml	orange juice
½	cup / 125	ml	port
½	cup / 125	ml	long grain rice
½	cup / 125	ml	wild rice
¼	cup / 50	ml	vinegar
1	tbsp / 15	ml	cornstarch
1	tbsp / 15	ml	water

salt & pepper to taste

Method

Wash mallard duck in cold water and wash inside cavity. Drain and pat dry. Season with salt and pepper. Place in roasting pan and cook in a moderate oven (375°F) for thirty minutes. Take off heat and remove the drippings from the pan. Set bird to the side.

Prepare your Rice

Put the wild rice in a small saucepan and fill with water just to cover. Set on top of the grate under campfire coals (or on top of the stove.) Bring to a boil and lower to a simmer. Let cook for twenty minutes or until the wild rice swells. Do the same with the long grain rice. Mix each rice together and add one tablespoon of butter. Salt and pepper to taste. Let become completely cool.

Place the rice mixture inside the cavity of the bird. Place back in the roaster and let cook for two hours.

Prepare the Sauce

Put the butter in a sauce pan and place on top of the grate over campfire coals. Swirl the butter around the pan until it begins to sizzle. Add the sugar and let it caramelize. Remove from heat. Cut four oranges in half and squeeze into the pan with pulp, but no seeds. Score the remanding two oranges and place the rind in the pan. Add the port and mix together. Bring back to the heat and mix in the orange juice, vinegar and the drippings. Thicken with a cornstarch base (cold water and cornstarch mixed together.) Cook for five minutes.

When the bird is cooked, take out and carve your favorite piece . First, place the wild rice in the middle of the plate. Add a piece of the bird and generously pour over the sauce. A rustic hunter's approaches to great cooking—enjoy!

In the late 1990's I had an acreage. In the back of my acreage I had a fairly good sized garden. Just behind my garden was a dense forest of spruce and willow trees.

It was just the beginning of spring and I was eager to start my garden. Out I went with my tractor to start plowing up the ground. As I started up my small tractor, I heard a great rumble in the thick forest. Out of the forest came crashing a bull moose, a little annoyed for waking him up. It startled me so much; I fell off my small tractor and raced for the house.

If the tractor wasn't in the way, I wouldn't be telling you this story today. For a minute there, I thought I was going to be minced meat pie! Talking about pies, here is a great recipe …

Tourtiere Moose Pies & Kinnikinnick Berries

I usually prepare these pies ahead, and then freeze them. Then they are ready for my hiking trip.

Yield: 4 servings

Ingredients

8	leaves		filo pastry
¼	cup / 50	ml	butter
¼	cup / 50	ml	olive oil
1	clove garlic		minced
¼	cup / 50	ml	flour
2	cups / 500	ml	kinnikinnick berries
½	cup / 125	ml	sugar
¼	cup / 50	ml	port
8	leaves		plantain
2	cups / 500	ml	moose stew meat
2	cups / 500	ml	venison stock
¼	cup / 50	ml	red wine
1	while		potato, small cut

1 whole carrot, small cut
salt & pepper to taste

Method

Pour the olive oil into a saucepan, and place on top of the stove. Heat the oil and place in the moose meat. Stir until brown on all sides. Add the minced garlic and stir. Stir in the flour and cook until a light brown or hazelnut taste. Add one cup of stock and red wine. Stir and let simmer for 30 minutes. Add the carrots and potato and let cook for 15 minutes. Salt and pepper to taste. Set to the side and let cool.

In a frying pan add berries and port. Flambé. Place in the sugar and put on the grate over medium heat. Cook until thickened. Let cool.

Take the filo pastry and set out on a cutting board. The pastry should be a square formation. If not, cut into an even square. Take the butter and melt it.

Brush a touch of the butter on the filo pastry. Take a second piece of filo pastry and place it on top of the first. Again, lightly brush it. Repeat, using all leaves of filo

Lay the two plantain leaves on top of the filo pastry. Spoon the berry mixture along the length of the plantain. Place a small portion of moose stew, again down the length. Roll the pastry, closing in the ends at the same time. Roll completely into a long cylinder. Place in the oven and let cook at 400°F until golden brown, approximately eight minutes—depending on the oven. And there you have it—another great treat!

Substitutions
Moose stew meat— beef stew meat

Entrées

Ptarmigan Piccata & Herb-buttered Tagliatelli

This entrée is best prepared at home or at the cottage

Yield: 4 servings

Ingredients

Piccata

4	whole		ptarmigan breasts
4	whole		eggs
1	cup / 250	ml	33% cream
¾	cup / 175	ml	flour
¼	cup / 50	ml	olive oil

Tagliatelli

2½ cups / 625		ml	flour
3	whole		eggs
1	tbsp / 15	ml	olive oil
1	fresh sprig		basil
3	cloves		garlic, minced
1	tbsp / 15	ml	butter

salt & pepper to taste

parmesan cheese to taste

Method
Piccata

Take the ptarmigan breasts and place in between plastic wrap. Pound out with a wooden mallet (or your favorite stone!)

Crack the eggs and pour the cream into a stainless steel bowl and mix well. Put flour in another bowl by itself. Add salt and pepper to taste.

Add the ptarmigan breasts to the flour and dredge well on both sides. Dip in the egg mix and again coat well.

Heat a frying pan with the ¼ cup olive oil on top of a grate on the campfire or on top of the stove.

Place the dredged ptarmigan in the hot oil and brown on both sides to a nice golden color.

Move to a cooking pan and place in a pre heated oven at 350 degrees. Cook at an even heat for twenty minutes, or until the bird is done.

Tagliatelli

Place flour on a board and make a well in the middle. Crack your eggs into the middle and add a pinch of salt. Form into stiff dough, adding water if required.

Roll out the dough to a thickness of $^{1}/_{16}$ " (thin). Cut into strips of ⅛" width and place out to dry.

Place the tablespoon of olive oil, fresh basil, butter and garlic into a frying pan. Melt on top of the stove or under the coals of the campfire. Set to the side.

Take a medium size pot with water and a pinch of salt. Place it on top the stove. Bring to a boil and add your dry homemade noodles. Cook until al dente.

Entrees

Place in bowl and toss with the olive oil and fresh basil mixture.

To the Plate

Plate the tagliatelli and top with ptarmigan piccata and fresh grated parmesan cheese. Season to taste.

Add a sprig of fresh basil on top and enjoy!

Substitutions

Ptarmigan breasts—chicken breasts

Chateaubriand Stuffed with Portabella Mushrooms

With roasted potatoes & honey glazed carrots

Yield: 8 servings

Ingredients
Chateaubriand

16 oz /500 g	venison or moose tenderloin (center cut)
3 cups/750 ml	portabella mushrooms (rough cut)
¼ cup/50ml	olive oil
1 small	onion, small cut
2 cloves	minced garlic
2 cups/500ml	cubed bread
¼ cup/50ml	venison stock
1 whole	egg
2 tsp/10ml	rosemary leaf (ground)
salt & pepper	to taste

Roast Potatoes

4 large	potatoes (cut into eight pieces)
½ cup/125ml	olive oil
1 tbsp/15ml	paprika
1 tbsp/15ml	garlic powder
1 tbsp/15ml	seasoning salt
½ tsp/15ml	black pepper
½ tsp/15ml	Cajun spice

Honey Glazed Carrots

8   carrots
(rough cut – ask chef bari for this term at http://chefbari.com)
2 tbsp/30ml   honey
1 tbsp/15ml   butter
1 tsp/5ml   dill weed

Preparing the Chateaubriand

Heat a frying pan on top of the grate under your campfire coals. Add half of the olive oil, along with the portabella mushrooms, onions and garlic. Sauté for a couple of minutes. Add the bread cubes and sauté for another couple of minutes. Place in stainless steel bowl (or metal bowl.) Add stock, egg and salt and pepper to taste. Mix together. Set to the side.

Take the center cut of the tenderloin and oil it with the other half of the oil. Rub in the rosemary, along with the salt and pepper. Place in hot frying pan and sear all sides. Move to a cutting board. Cut down the length of the tenderloin and place in the stuffing. Roll up tight and tie with string. Place in reflector oven at moderate heat or in regular oven at 350°F. Cook for 25 minutes or until your liking.

Preparing the Roast Potatoes

Place all of the seasonings, herbs and oil in a mixing bowl. Add your medium cut potatoes. Mix together until well coated. Strain potatoes out of oil mixture and place on baking sheet. Make sure it is well strained. Place in the reflector oven at moderate heat or regular oven at 350°F. Let cook for 30 minutes until tender.

Preparing Honey Glazed Carrots

Place a medium size pot with water on top of the grate under coals of your campfire. Add the carrots and bring to a boil. Cook until tender. Take off and drain water. Add cold water to stop cooking process. Drain and pat dry.
In a frying pan, put in the butter and honey and set on top of the grate. When melted, add the carrots and dill. Sauté for five minutes.

To the Plate

In the center of a large oval plate, place your cooked chateaubriand. Around the chateaubriand, mix together the carrots and potatoes. Add a fresh sprig of rosemary leaf on each side of oval plate. Viola—bon appetite! Very tasty with béarnaise sauce.

Substitutions

Moose or venison tenderloin— Beef tenderloin

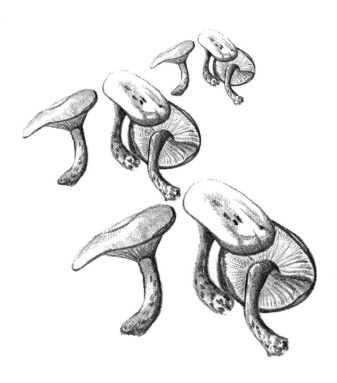

Entrees

Madagascar Entrecote

With parisenne dill potatoes & roasted corn on the cob

This entrée is best prepared at home, at the cottage or a public campsite.

Yield: 4 servings

Ingredients

Entrecote

4 8oz / 250 g sirloin venison or moose steaks
½ cup / 125 ml Madagascar peppercorns (green peppercorns), crushed
½ cup / 125 ml red wine
¼ onion, finely chopped
2 cloves garlic, minced
¼ cup / 50 ml olive oil
salt & pepper to taste

Parisenne Dill Potatoes & Roasted Corn on the Cob

6 whole potatoes, peeled
1 tbsp / 15 ml dill weed
¼ cup / 50 ml olive oil
4 whole corns on the cob
4 tbsp / 45 ml butter, melted
salt & pepper to taste

Method
Entrecote
Rub some of the olive oil on the steaks and season well. Pour the rest of the olive oil in a frying pan and place on top of the stove. When the pan is hot, place in the steaks and sear both sides. Take out and place to the side.

Add the onions, garlic and crushed green peppercorns to the frying pan. Sauté for a couple of minutes and add red wine. Let reduce and add the steaks back into the sauce. Cook until done.

Parisienne Dill Potatoes & Roasted Corn on the Cob
Take the peeled potatoes and with melon ball, dig into raw potatoes to form small golf balls.

In a mixing bowl, add ½ of the melted butter with all of the olive oil. Sprinkle in the dill and mix.

Add the golf ball potatoes and mix.

Place on baking sheet and put in the oven at 350°F until tender, approximately 25 minutes.

Cook the corn in hot water until tender. Drain and place corn directly on top of the grate to barbecue. When you have marked all sides of the corn, place in tin foil and cover the rest of the butter and season to taste. Cover with the tin foil and place in reflector oven or in your barbecue. Let roast for ten minutes.

To the Plate
Take the steaks and place in the middle of the plate. Drizzle the Madagascar peppercorn sauce on top. Place Parsienne potatoes along side of the steak. And along side of the potatoes, add the corn. You are ready to enjoy a favorite of mine.

Substitutions
Moose or Venison steak— Beef Sirloin or New York Cut steak

Yukon Gold Miner's Chili

There is nothing better than enjoying a plateful of hot chili out on the trail. You can either prepare this dish ahead of time or out on the trail. If you do decide to prepare this meal out on the trail, it is best to cook the ground hamburger (in this case, ground bison) before you leave.

Here is my version of chili.

Yield: 4 servings

Ingredients

2	lbs	/ 1	kg	ground buffalo
2	tbsp	/ 30	ml	olive oil
1	whole			onion, chopped
1	tbsp	/ 30	ml	garlic, chopped
2	tbsp	/ 30	ml	chili powder
1	tsp	/ 5	ml	dried chilies
1	cup	/ 250	ml	Black beans
1	cup	/ 250	ml	pork & beans
¼	lb	/ 125	g	bacon, chopped
2	tsp	/ 10	ml	salt
2	tsp	/ 10	ml	black pepper
2	tbsp	/ 30	ml	paprika
1	whole			jalapeno pepper
2	cups	/ 500	ml	tomato sauce
½	cup	/ 125	ml	tomato paste
2	cups	/ 500	ml	water

Method

Place the oil in a medium size pot and heat. Add bacon and cook until almost crispy, take out the bacon and add your ground bison (ground buffalo meat) and cook until well done.

Add the cooked bacon, chopped onion, garlic, chili powder, salt, black pepper, paprika and dried chilies. Sauté for ten minutes on medium heat, mixing with a wooden spoon.

> Finely chop the fresh jalapeno pepper and add to dish. Pour in the tomato sauce and paste. Mix well and lower heat. Sauté on low heat for 45 minutes, adding water each time it becomes dry.
>
> This dish is best the next day, because all the flavours intensify into one great chili! Serve with a fresh bun or loaf of French bread.

Time for Dessert!

Desserts

Nothing better to finish off a gourmet meal with a yummy dessert! Before I head into the wilderness I make up a batch of desserts to take on the trip. Or you can make these at your favorite cottage retreat.
Here is a selection from my sweet tooth.

Grizzly Bear Claws

Ingredients

1 whole egg
1 cup / 250 ml butter
¾ cup / 175 ml sugar
1 tbsp / 15 ml vanilla
1 cup / 250 ml chocolate chips
2½ cups / 625 ml flour
2½ tsp baking powder
½ tsp baking soda

Method

Place one cup of butter in a bowl (preferably a metal bowl) and whip to a nice creamy white color. Gently add in the sugar and the eggs. Again whip until well mixed.

Add together flour, baking powder & baking soda in a separate bowl. Mix flour mixture to above cream mixture, but be careful not to over mix...

Divide into four pieces and roll out to ½ inch thickness. Cut each rolled section into eight 3 inch half-moon shapes. Cover with a cloth and let rest for ten minutes.

Place in preheated oven at 350°F for twenty minutes. Bring out and let cool.

while the grizzly bear claws are cooling...

Ingredients:

1 cup / 250 ml unsweetened chocolate chips
1 tbsp / 15 ml butter
1 pkg gelatin
1 tbsp / 15 ml brandy
¼ cup / 50 ml water

Method

In a double boiler, add the chocolate chips, butter & brandy. Mix until smooth. In a small container sprinkle gelatin over water and let stand for five minutes. Mix into the smooth hot chocolate until dissolved. Drizzle on top of the baked Grizzle Bear Claws as much or as little as you want.

This is great after a long or short hike!

Desserts

Rocky Mountain Cookie

Ingredients
Bottom Crust

1 cup / 250 ml graham crumbs   ½ cup / 125 ml melted butter

Filling

¾	cup / 175	ml	butter
1	cup / 250	ml	brown sugar
4	whole		eggs
1	tsp / 5	ml	vanilla
1	oz / 30	g	orange brandy
¼	cup / 50	ml	sliced almonds
	2½ cup / 635	ml	pecans

Method

Preheat oven to 325 F

Bottom Crust

Pour the melted butter in a bowl and mix in the graham crumbs. Spray the bottom and sides of a spring form pan with a vegetable coating spray.

Press the graham mixture into the bottom of the spring form pan. Place in oven for five minutes. Remove and let cool.

Filling

With your mixer, whip butter to a nice creamy white color. Gently add in the sugar, vanilla, brandy and eggs. Mix in the pecans & sliced almonds. Place on top of crust and place back in the oven at 350 F for thirty minutes. Let cool and cut into squares, wrap & freeze.

Cakes

When at home or at the cottage, I often spend my evenings cooking up my favorite cakes.

Chocolate Moose Canadian Cake

Ingredients
Bottom Crust:

1 cup / 250 ml graham crumbs
½ cup / 125 ml melted butter

White Chocolate Moose

8 oz / 250 g	cream cheese, cubed
2 cups / 500 ml	33% whipping cream
2 cups / 500ml	sweet white chocolate
2 pkg's	unflavored gelatin
½ cup / 125 ml	water

Decoration

1 cup / 250ml dark chocolate chips
1 tsp / 2 ml butter
¼ cup / 50 ml water
1 pkg gelatin

Method

bottom crust

Pour the melted butter in a bowl and mix in the graham crumbs. Spray the bottom and sides of a spring form pan with a vegetable coating spray.

Press the graham mixture into the bottom of the spring form pan. Place in a preheated oven at 325°F for five minutes. Remove from oven and let cool.

Desserts

White Chocolate Moose

In a mixer, add your cream cheese and 1 cup of whipping cream mix until combined.

In a double broiler, melt white chocolate. As this is melting, take a small saucepan and add your water. Sprinkle the gelatin over the water and come back to it in five minutes.

Heat the gelatin mixture on low heat and pour into the melted white chocolate; mix well.

You will require two metal bowls; one for the white chocolate mixture & a larger one for ice and water. Chill the chocolate mixture over the largest bowl with ice and 1/2 cup of water. Stir with wooden spoon until it begins to cool.

Take the other cup of whipping cream and mix until it reaches a stiff peak.

Fold whipped cream into cream cheese in mixer and then slowly fold in white chocolate mixture.

Spread on top of graham crust in the spring form pan and let set in fridge until firm.

Decoration

Melt the dark chocolate chips and butter in a double boiler.
While it is melting, place gelatin in water and let stand for five minutes. Heat up gelatin and place in double boiler. When well incorporated, take off heat and let cool.

Procedure:

Take the moose cake out of the fridge and remove the sides of the spring form pan. Place the dark chocolate mixture into a piping bag with a fine tube and begin to decorate. You can place many different designs of your choice or even make a picture of a moose on top of the cake. I like to drizzle the sides of the cake as well. This is where the fun is, you are in control, and **You are the artist!** Kids Enjoy taking part.

Wild Strawberry Cheesecake

Yield: 2 cheesecakes

Ingredients

Bottom Crust

1 cup / 250 ml graham crumbs
½ cup / 125 ml melted butter

Cream Cheese Filling

6 medium	eggs
½ cup / 125 ml	sour cream
3 lb / 1.5 kg	cream cheese (cut into cubes)
1½ cups / 375 ml	sugar
1 tsp / 5 ml	vanilla
½ tsp / 2 ml	lemon juice
1 cup / 250 ml	wild or farm strawberries (sliced)

Topping

1 cup / 250 ml	33% whipping cream
¼ cup / 125 ml	sugar
10 whole	strawberries

Strawberry Sauce

3 cups / 750 ml	wild or farm strawberries (sliced)
2 cups / 500 ml	sugar

Method
Bottom Crust

Pour the melted butter in a bowl and mix in the graham crumbs. Spray the bottom and sides of a spring form pan with a vegetable coating spray.

Press the graham mixture into the bottom of the spring form pan.
Bake in a preheated oven at 325°F for five minutes. Remove and let cool.

Cream Cheese Filling

Whip the cream cheese in the mixer until smooth. Add one egg at a time and mix well until all are incorporated.

Blend in the rest of the ingredients and mix well. Pour into the spring form pan and place in preheated oven at 300°F for 45–55 minutes, until the cheesecake has a cracked line in the middle. Take out and place in the fridge for 20 minutes to cool.

Toppings

Whip the cream until it begins to form a peak; slowly adding
the sugar. Place the whipping cream in a pastry bag and form 10 florets along the outside edges of the cheesecake.

Place a fresh strawberry on top of the whipping cream.

Strawberry Sauce

Heat ingredients in a saucepan they form a syrup Enjoy!

Home Sweet Home

NOTES

home sweet home

It is always great to get outdoors, but it is also nice to be home. You come home to running water, heat, electricity—the essentials.

Well, that is what you think when you leave. When you arrive home, you feel like a new person after that first shower and the comfort of your warm bed. Another comfort is to be able to use the modern technology of microwaves, ovens, dishwashers and fridges.

With all the convenience of home, you can easily prepare these next two recipes for that special gourmet meal.

Tequila Lime Chicken & Shrimp Fettuccine

Yield: 4 servings

Ingredients

¼	cup / 50	ml	olive oil
1	cup / 250	ml	mushrooms
½	cup / 125	ml	red peppers, chopped
1	tsp / 5	ml	garlic, minced
6	oz / 170	g	raw chicken breast, cubed
1	oz / 30	g	tequila
½	fresh		lime
2	cups / 500	ml	33% whipping cream
½	cup / 125	ml	raw jumbo shrimp, peeled
4	cups / 1	litre	cooked fettuccine

Method

Take out your favorite deep sauté pan and set it on top of the stove. Add the olive oil and turn heat to medium high. Let the oil become hot (not smoking) and add the mushrooms, sauté for a couple of minutes. Remove pan from heat.

Add the raw cubed chicken breast and let cook for five minutes, stirring mixture off and on.

Add the raw shrimp and minced garlic to the pan and sauté for four minutes.

Take the pan off the burner and flambé with tequila. Return to stove and squeeze lime juice into the pan. Add the whipping cream and parmesan cheese.

Add the cooked fettuccine to the pan, lower the heat to a simmer and let cook until it begins to pull away from the pan.

Arrange fettuccine dish in your favourite pasta bowl and enjoy.

Goes great with garlic toast!

Here is a fast easy way of preparing a dish that you have spent very little money on, and no one can tell the difference. Instead of using the authentic Cornish game hens, you can substitute a double breast of chicken (this simply means that both sides of the breast are intact.)

Canadian Style Cornish Game Hen with Shitake Mushrooms Sauce

Yield: 2 servings

Ingredients

2	pieces		double breast chicken with leg bone still attached
4	tbsp / 60	ml	olive oil
½	cup / 125	ml	wild rice
½	cup / 125	ml	long grain rice
2	cups / 500	ml	water
2	cups / 500	ml	shitake mushrooms
1	tsp / 5	ml	garlic, minced
2	cups / 500	ml	chicken stock
2	tbsp / 30	ml	butter
2	tbsp / 30	ml	flour
½	cup / 125	ml	33% whipping cream

salt & pepper to taste

Method

Preparing the Rice

Place the wild rice in a small saucepan and fill with water just to cover. Set on top of the grate under campfire coals (or on top of the stove.) Bring to a boil and lower to a simmer. Let cook for twenty minutes or until the wild rice swells.

Do the same with the long grain rice.

Mix each rice together and add one tablespoon of butter. Salt and pepper to taste. Cool completely.

preparing the chicken

Lay the double breast of chicken on a flat surface. Remove the tender from inside (you can't miss it; it looks like a chicken finger.) Place a sheet of plastic liner on top of the breast.

Take a mallet and flatten the breast slightly. Add the rice mixture with two tablespoons of olive oil in the middle of the chicken, forming an oval ball shape. Season with salt and pepper. Roll up the chicken carefully and fold together. (See Diagram on page 98.)

Tie with butcher twine and place on a baking sheet. Place on a covered baking sheet, season with salt and pepper and bake in a pre-heated oven at 350°F for fifty minutes.

preparing the sauce:

Add the butter to a saucepan and let melt. Stir in the shitake mushrooms and sauté.

Stir in the flour on low heat. Place your chicken stock in the microwave for one minute. Slowly mix into the saucepan.

Warm up your 33% cream in the microwave as well for thirty seconds. Slowly mix this into the saucepan. Let simmer on low heat for ten minutes.

To the Plate

On your best china, drizzle on half of the sauce in the middle. Lay the cooked Canadian Cornish Game Hen on top of the sauce.

Pour the rest of the sauce on one side of the chicken. You can-serve this with my roast potatoes (page 71) and a Caesar Salad (page 40).

Bon appetite! Fast and easy!

home sweet home

Canadian Style Cornish Game Hen Assembly

In the supermarket ask your butcher for a double breasted chicken with the legs and skin attached. You will require the skin to keep the bird together. But after the cooking process you may remove the skin if you like.

If you are confused about this procedure you are welcome to join myself for a private cooking class. Just contact me at bari@chefbari.com for further information. Please have a look at the diagram on page 98. A picture is worth a thousand words – as they say.

http://chefbari.com

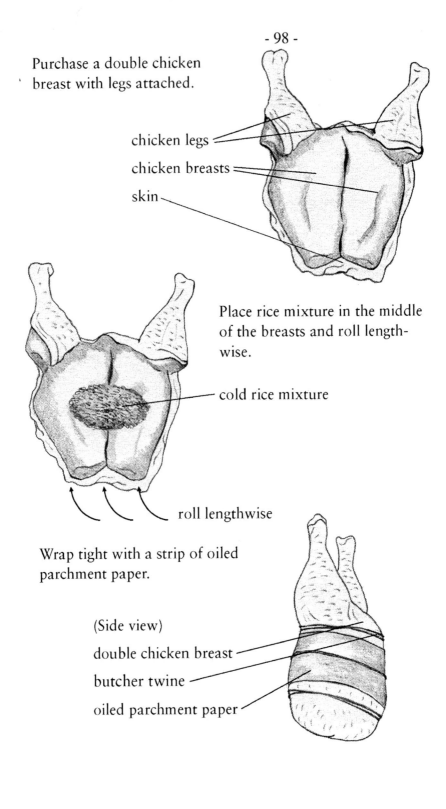

NOTES:

Canadian Northwest Company Division

The Canadian Northwest Company Division was developed to inform its customers the need to help the sick children in Canada. In 2007, this book started to place 50% of its funds towards children's charities to help research and development. Even though other children (like my child, Jenni) were not fortunate enough to receive the help in time, there is still hope for those little miracles today. Thank you for supporting our children for today and the future.

With your help, it is my hope to have such items as: Authentic Canadian Northwest tee shirts, hats, other books and related items to continue on with research and development for children. Please have a look at http://chefbari.com for updates. If your company can donate to support sick children, please contact bari@chefbari.com

Conservationist Corner

The most important lesson when taking C.O.R.E. (Conservation Outdoor Recreation Education) is how to become a safe outdoorsman. You learn how to control what is around you and to be aware of the habits of the game that you seek. With this knowledge, you can enjoy the wilderness and not be intimidated by it.

As conservationists, we can become an important part of the ecological system or we can destroy it. To best understand ecology, you must understand what it means. Ecology plays an important role in controlling the very delicate balance of nature. If we destroy a part of our environment, we destroy a part of ourselves. Being aware of this, man already being a part of the ecological system, can be a part of the population control of our wildlife.

Too many times you hear the horror of poachers that kill our wildlife, just so they can sell their organs. Fortunately, our Fish and Wildlife Management Units are very aware of this kind of destruction.

As concerned conservationists, we can become a very important part in making sure that poaching stops. Working together as a team, we can help Fish and Wildlife Management fight to preserve our wildlife.

So, if you are out in your neck-of-the-woods and you see something that is not right, fight back by phoning your local Fish and Wildlife Branch. Let's protect our wildlife, so our children's children can enjoy them too.

About the Author

Chef Bari Demers was born and raised in Edmonton, Alberta for his first ten years. Then he moved to Vernon, British Columbia, and that was the beginning of his adventure!

As an avid outdoorsman, Bari volunteered with the Vernon Fish and Wildlife Club. To encourage his understanding of wildlife, he took his training with C.O.R.E. (Conservation Outdoor Recreation Education.)

Bari's love for the outdoors left him many times cooking around a campfire —and boy, did he cook up a storm!

So, he decided to go back to the city of Edmonton to obtain his cooking Culinary Expertise. With three years at N.A.I.T. (Northern Alberta Institute of Technology), Chef Bari became the Top Third Year Apprentice of the C.C.F.C.C., the Canadian Culinary Federation/Federation Culinary Canadienne. He worked at the top hotels in the city and participated in the World Class Culinary Art Exhibition, where he brought home a bronze medal for best served dishes in the **Entrée Class**.

He went back to British Columbia to work as Executive Chef of Kelowna Springs, where his creativity grew. After this, it was time to begin his own company. **The Canadian Northwest Company Division** was born.

Presently, Chef Bari Demers is concentrating on helping the **Stollery Children's Hospital Foundation** to further research for the sick children.

NOTES:

Canadian Northwest Company Glossary

A

Asparagus. Thin green or white long edible vegetable that some might say it resembles a paintbrush.

Assiniboine. A North American Native tribe called the Assiniboine established the jagged peak of Mount Assiniboine as their home. Unknown to most was that this home land region was also home to the Klunaxa as well. The Assiniboine Tribe is also known as the Stoney Plain Tribe.

B

Bannock. A quick dough method bread item made by trappers and homesteaders in North America

Béarnaise sauce. Hollandaise sauce with tarragon vinegar added to it.

Blueberry. An edible round blue berry used for pies, sauces, desserts, jams & jellies
Buffalo berry. An edible round reddish berry that has a very thick consistency when cook. Again, great for pies, sauces, desserts, jams & jellies

Raspberry. An edible oval seedy red berry great for all food items
Salmonberry. A very common wild berry found in moist area's in the wilderness. A broad dull red berry that highly resembles the raspberry plant.
Bella Coola. A West Coast Native tribe of British Columbia
Buffalo. A beautiful endangered animal that much resembles your everyday cow, but with a greater distinction of power and pride. Very unfortunate
during the 1800's, man slaughtered millions of these beautiful animals, just so they could control the Native Tribes of North America. Most unfortunate part of man's history.

C

Camembert. A creamy white cheese that is accessible in any supermarket.

Canadian Northwest Company Division. A company committed to donate 50 % of its funds towards the Stollery Children's Hospital Foundation and other sick Children fund raisers. If you have a children's fund raiser that will help the interest of children's culture, history and welfare in Canada, please contact Chef Bari Demers at bari@chefbari.com or http://chefbari.com

Chef Bari is is a food lover's guide. It also is a tool in helping your children in health care to have a healthy lifestyle.

Consultant Services from Resorts, Hotels to Restaurants

Do Not Spend Another Dime Without Checking With Me First! - I will save You Money!

Services Available:

1. Consultation on Resorts, Hotels or Restaurants of Your Choice - Don't Go to another Resort just to be disappointed again. I guaranteed Satisfaction as to your request.

2. Restaurant Kitchen Design and layout - includes menu design and planning, with complete mise en place, hiring of staff and dry run. Do exactly what the corporate companies are doing for half the cost and expenses.

3. Private Cooking Classes Consultation Designed to Your Specifications - great for birthdays, events, bbq's, anniversaries, corporate events or the girls night out.

Contact bari@chefbari.com for further information or go to www.chefbari.com

We offer a free Gourmet Fun in the Sun Club that is available to everyone across the world. All you have to do is go to http://chefbari.com to join up.

Chanterelle mushroom. A wild edible mushroom found in most dense wilderness forests close to the mountains. A picture explains it:

Chateaubriand. A beef of tenderloin that can be purchased in any super

market. Hunter's favorite and most tender part of wild game.

Chilcotin. A British Columbia native tribe that lives in the interior of British Columbia

Chowder. A thick creamy soup base

Cree. A Plains native tribe that lives from British Columbia to as far as Manitoba and the United States.

D

Dandelion. A broad leaf plant that is very common to most house holds in North America. When the plant is young, its leaves are very tender & edible. But once they grow to mature stage, they become bitter.

Dijon mustard. Grainy seed mustard that originated in France. The original has French white wine mixed with the mustard. Today, there are hundreds of different types to choose from.

Demi-glace. A basic thick brown sauce that is mixed with beef stock and Madeira or sherry.

E

Entrecote. A French term that literally means "between the ribs". Ask your butcher for a cut from the 9th to 11th part of the ribs of meat. When you take the bone off, you get what is called the New York Strip loin. When cut into slices, this is very common to everyone, the New York\ Steak

F

Fiddlehead. A member of the fern family of plants. When very young it comes out of the ground like the shape of a fiddle head. Therefore, this is where the name comes from. It is bright green and after ascertains stage becomes very bitter and inedible.

Filo dough. A very thin piece of flaky dough that you now can buy in the frozen section of your supermarket.

G

Grouse (blue). A wild bird that is found all over North America. Common for hunters to gather for food around the camp.

Inside round. As the word implies, it is the inside part of the beef or wild game; around the hip area.

J

Jalapeno. A spicy pepper that is now very common throughout supermarkets.

K

Kinnickinnick. Also known as bearberry; it is a very common, low, bushy, green mat that love the dense, moist forest. It has very small, green shiny leaves and very bright red berries. The native tribes used the leaves for various medicine remedies and for tobacco. The red berries were used for jerky, drink and today it is used for jams and jellies.

L
Leek. Another common vegetable plant that resembles a very large green onion.
M
Madagascar. A term used for the type of small green pepper, which adds very nice flavour to your meal.

Marinate. To soak meat or vegetable for a period of time to let the juices absorb the flavour of the ingredients that you use in a marinade.

Mushrooms. See chanterelle, shitake, portabella

Moose. A very large wild animal that is very common throughout Canada. A picture tells a million words:

O
Olive oil. A common oil used in Italy, Greece and other very hot regions of the world. Extremely common in all supermarkets throughout North America.
P
Pesto. A mixture of pine nuts, olive oil, salt and fresh basil blended to

gether. Used for sauces, pasta's and other gourmet dishes.

Piccatta. A special dish, where you dip the meat into an egg mixture and fried on the grill.

Plantain. A broad leaf plant that is similar to the dandelion plant.

R

Rainbow trout. A special fresh water fish that sides resembles colors of the rainbow. A great fun catch and tasty to eat.

Reflector oven. A quick assemble tin oven that is found in any outdoor store.

Rosemary leaf. An herb that is used in food items to bring out more dis tinct flavour.

S

Salmonberry. See **Berries**.

Spinach. A common broad leaf plant that is as a dark rich green colour.

Sprig. A touch of….. A pinch of ….or can also be known as a tip of a plant

spring form pan. A round pan with high, straight sides (2 1/2 to 3 inches) that expand with the aid of a spring or clamp. The separate bottom of the pan can be removed from the sides when the clamp is released.

Stoney Plain. A native tribe in Alberta that is also known as Assiniboine. See **Assiniboine**.

T

Tagliatelli. This is an Italian term used for broad long pasta, that re sembles very much like fettuccine.

Tenderloin. A special side of beef that can be purchased at any supermarket. Just ask your butcher.

Tourtiere. A French-Canadian style of meat pie.

V

Venison. This common name is used for deer meat.

Violaˆ. A French term meaning "there you are" or "there it is"

W

Wild. Living without commercial help by man.

Index

A Almonds
sliced 83 **al dente** 21, 53, 63, 69 **Appetizers** 14

B

Bannock 19, 105 **Barbecue**
Bbq 52 **barbecue** 23, 43, 53, 75
Barley 31
Basil 45, 46, 51, 52, 53, 87
Bbq 52 **Bear** 42, vii
Bearnaise 105
Beef 18, 23, 29, 31, 54, 66, 73, 75, 106,107
Bella Coola 17, 105
Berries
Buffalo with Kinnickinnick Berry 17 Rainbow Trout Stuffed with Long Grain Rice & Buffalo Berries 59 salmonberries 58
  Crisp Blue Grouse Breasts and Salmonberry Demi-glaze 55
Tourtiere Moose Pies & Kinnikinnick Berries 65
Bison 76
Blackfoot 17
Blueberry 105
Vinaigrette 42
Blue Grouse
Blue Grouse Stock 32
Cajun Blue Grouse Fingers 20
Crisp Blue Grouse Breasts and Salmonberry Demi-glaze 55
grouse

  stock used in recipe 33
  Buffalo 17
  buffalo inside round 17
  substitutions for 18
Buffalo with Kinnikinnick Berry 17
substitution for 18
Yukon Gold Miner's Chili 76

Buffalo berry
Rainbow Trout stuffed with Wild Rice & Buffalo Berries 59

Buffalo jerky 17

C

C.C.F.C.C. 103
C.O.R.E 100
Caesar Dressing 40
Caesar Salad 60
Wilderness Caesar
Salad 40

Cajun
Cajun Blue Grouse Fingers 20
Cajun spice 20, 23, 53, 55, 71
Cake 84
Canadian Chocolate Moose Cake 84
Wild Strawberry Cheesecake 86
Camembert 24, 33, 34, 106
Campfire

cooking on 17, 21, 29, 30, 52, 53, 55, 57, 58 63,64, 69,72, 94, 103

Canadian Recipes iii, vii
Canadian Wilderness vii
Chanterelle. See Mushrooms: chanterelle
Chanterelle Mushrooms vii
Bbq Moose Tenderloin &ChanterelleMushrooms 52
sauce 54
using wild 53
Chateaubriand 106
Chateaubriand Stuffed with PortabellaMushrooms 71
Cheese
Camembert 24, 33, 34, 106
cheddar 19
cream cheese
Wild Strawberry Cheesecake 86
parmesan 21. 22, 40, 42, 43, 45,

Swiss 30
Cheesecake. See **Cake:** **Wild Strawberry Cheesecake**
Chicken
  breast 92 preparation as mock game
  hen 95 Canadian Style Cornish
  Game Hen with Shitake Mushrooms
  Sauce 94 substitutions for blue
  grouse bones 20

  Blue grouse breasts 20, 58
  blue grouse strips 20
  Ptarmigan breasts 70

Tequila Lime Chicken Fettuccine 92
 Chilcotin 17, 106
Chili 19
 Yukon Gold Miner's Chili 76
Chocolate
 Chocolate Moose Canadian Cake 84
 white 84
 white chocolate moose 84

Chowder 106 Dolly Varden Chowder 35
Cinnamon
 Honey Cinnamon Moose Tenderloin 23
 Conservationist 100
 Corn
 roasted corn on the cob 74, 75
Cornish game hen
 Canadian Style Cornish Game Hen with Shitake Mushrooms Sauce 94
Cream Cheese
Chocolate Moose Canadian Cake 84
Wild Strawberry Cheesecake 86

Cree 17, 106

D

Dandelion 40, 42, 45, 106, 109 **Demi-glaze** 106
Crisp Blue Grouse
Breasts and Salmonberry
Demi-glaze
Dessert 78/79 Chocolate Moose Canadian Cake 84 Grizzly Bear Claws 81
 Rocky Mountain Cookie 83

Wild Strawberry Cheesecake 86
Dijon mustard 40, 55
Dill 35, 52, 53, 59, 60, 71, 72, 74, 75
Dolly Varden
  Dolly Varden Chowder 35

E

Ecology 100
Edmonton 65, 103, 106
Entrecote
  Madagascar Entrecote 74

F

Fettuccine 21, 92, 93, 110
  substitutions
    tagliatelli 22

Fiddleheads 58
  Wild Fiddlehead Soup 33
  with Crisp Blue Grouse Breasts 55

Filo 49, 50
Fish and Wildlife Management 100
Fish Bones 35
Fish Stock 35
Flambé 66, 93
Forest 65
French 110

  bread 77
  Canadian French Onion & Wild Leek Soup 30
  Dijon mustard 106
  entrecote 107
  Tourtiere 110

Frenchman River 59

G

German Pan-fried Potatoes 52, 54, vii
Graham crumbs 84, 86
Grizzly

  Grizzly Bear Claws 81
Ground bison 76
ground buffalo 76

H

Hazelnut 66 **Home** 17, 18, 21, 29, 42, 59, 60,63,68, 84, 92 vii
Homemade noodles
  Herb buttered Tagliatelli
    method 69
    Tagliatelli con Dente di
  Leone
    method 21
    Tagliatelli con Pesto
    method 63

Honey
  Honey Cinnamon Moose Tenderloin 23
  Honey Glazed Carrots 71
  Honey glazed carrots
  Http://chefbari.com 79

  preparation 72
Hunter's 64chateaubriand 106 Hunter's Roasted Mallard Duck a l'orange
  stuffed with Wild Rice 63
Hunters
  Grouse (blue) 107

I **Inside Round**
  Buffalo 17
  substitutions 18

J

Jalapeno 76, 77

Jerky 17

L

Leek 29, 31, 32, 33, 52, 53, 55, 57
Lettuces
  Romaine
    substitutions 41

M

Madagascar 108 Madagascar Entrecote 74 Madagascar peppercorns 74 Madagascar peppercorn sauce 75

Mallard
Hunter's Roasted Mallard Duck a l'orange
  stuffed with Wild Rice 63
Marinated Mallard Duck Salad with Blueberry Vinaigrette 42
substitutions 43

Medallions
Fresh venison vii
Moose 108 Bbq Moose Tenderloin & Chanterelle Mushrooms 52 Chocolate Moose Canadian Cake. See Cake: Canadian Chocolate
  Moose Cake
Honey Cinnamon Moose Tenderloin 23
substitutions

  Moose or venison steak 75
    Moose or venison tenderloin 73
    Tourti re Moose Pies & Kinnikinnick
    Berries 65 **Mountain** vii Rocky
    Mountain Cookie. See Dessert: Rocky
    Mountain Cookie **Mushrooms** 92, vii
    chanterelle 106 Bbq Moose
    Tenderloin & Chanterelle Mushrooms
    52 Note re: wild chanterelle
    mushrooms 53 portabella 72
    Chateaubriand Stuffed with Portabella
    Mushrooms 71 shitake Canadian Style
    Cornish Game Hen with Shitake
    Mushrooms Sauce 94

N

National Parks vii
New York Cut steak

  substitutions 75
Northwest
Canadian Northwest Company 100, 103, 106

O

      Okanagan 17, 24, 42
      Olive oil 17, 18, 21, 31, 33, 35, 40, 42, 43, 45,
      52, 53, 55, 57, 59, 60, 61, 63, 65, 66, 68, 69, 70,
      71, 72, 74, 75, 76, 92, 94, 95, 109
Orange
  Hunter's Roasted Mallard Duck ˆ l'orange
  stuffed with Wild Rice 63 in sauce 64

    Orange Brandy 83

P

Parmesan. See Cheese: parmesan
Pastry

  philo. See philo
    method 50
  pastry bag 87
  peak 87

Pecans 83
Peppercorns

  black 35
  green 74, 75
  peppercorn sauce 75

Pies
Blueberry 105
buffalo berry 105
Tourti re Moose Pies & Kinnikinnick Berries 465

Plantain 40, 41, 45,

  baby plantain 41
  Port 63, 64, 66
  orange sauce 64
Portabella. See Mushrooms: portabella
Potatoes 31, 35, 52, vii German
  fried potatoes 54 Parisienne
  dill potatoes 75
    preparation 76
  roasted 71
    preparation 72
    with Canadian Style Cornish Game Hen 95

Ptarmigan
  Ptarmigan Piccata & Herb buttered
  Tagliatelli 68
  substitutions
  ptarmigan breasts 70

R

Rainbow trout, 59, 60, 110 preparation and cleaning 60 Rainbow Trout Stuffed with Long Grain Rice & Buffalo Berries 59

Raspberry 105
  substitutions 42 **Reflector oven** 24, 55, 60, 72, 75, 110
Rice
long grain rice 55, 57, 59, 63, 94
wild 64, 94
  Crisp Blue Grouse Breasts and Salmonberry Demi-glaze 55
  Hunter's Roasted Mallard Duck ˆ l'orange stuffed with Wild Rice

    63
preparation 57

Roasted corn. See Corn

Roast potatoes. See Potatoes: roasted

Romaine lettuce. See Lettuce

Rosemary leaf 29, 31, 55, 71, 72, 110

S

Salad 37, 43, 60, 95
Hiker's

Marinated Mallard Duck
  Salad with Blueberry
  Vinaigrette 42
  Wilderness Caesar
  Salad 40
    Salmon
      substitutions 36
    Salmonberry. See Berries: salmonberries
    Sauce 75
      béarnaise 73, 105
      chanterelle 53, 54
      demi-glaze 106
      dill 60
      kinnickinnick 17
      l'orange 63
      Madagascar peppercorn 74
      salmonberry 55
      shitake mushroom 95

        Canadian Style Cornish Game Hen with Shitake Mushrooms Sauce
          94
      strawberry 86, 87
      tomato 76, 77

    Sauté 21, 31, 33, 36, 53, 72, 92, 93, 95

Sear 72, 74
Shitake. See Mushrooms: shitake
Shrimp 92, 93
Shuswap Falls 42
Sirloin 74, 75
Soup 33

    Blue Grouse Stock 32
    Canadian French Onion & Wild Leek Soup 30
    chowder 106

    Dolly Varden Chowder 35
    Soups & Stocks 26
    Venison Barley Soup 31
    Venison Stock 29
    Wild Fiddlehead Soup 33

Spinach 110
  substitutions 22, 45

  Steak
beef
    substitutions 75
    entrecote 107

  Stew

Moose 65, 66
  substitutions 67

Stock
  Blue grouse 32, 33, 55, 57
  chicken 58
  demi-glaze

  beef 84
 fish 25, 26
 venison 29, 30, 31, 66, 71

Stoney Plain 17, 107, 110

T Tagliatelli
  homemade tagliatelli noodles
    method 21

Ptarmigan Piccata & Herb-buttered Tagliatelli 68
Tagliatelli con Dente di Leone 21
Tagliatelli con Pesto 61

Thompson 17

Venison 110, vii. **See Stock: venison** bones
   substitution 29
   cubed 31
   sirloin 74
   stock 30, 65
   substitutions 31
   tenderloin 71

    substitutions 73
Venison Barley Soup. See Soup: Venison Barley Soup
Vinaigrette
  Marinated Mallard Duck Salad with Blueberry Vinaigrette 42 method 43

W

White chocolate moose 84
  method 84
  White wine 32, 42, 43, 59, 60, 106
  Wild
   asparagus 37, 38, 39
   Baked Camembert and Wild Asparagus 24
   mix greens 42, 43, 45

   substitutions 45.44.41,36.
  pine nuts 61, 63, 109
  rice 55, 64, 94

   method 56
   preparation 47
Wilderness Caesar Salad 40
  http://chefbari.com 100
   http://gourmetsuntours.com
   http://hikingmania.com
   http://chefbari.com
   bari@chefbari.com